Why Trees?
How to Love Trees

By Martin R. Ford

 FriesenPress

One Printers Way
Altona, MB R0G 0B0
Canada

www.friesenpress.com

ISBN
978-1-03-918286-8 (Hardcover)
978-1-03-918285-1 (Paperback)
978-1-03-918287-5 (eBook)

1. NATURE, PLANTS, TREES

Distributed to the trade by The Ingram Book Company

This book is dedicated to all people living in cities.

Cover photo: Elm tree living on Alice Street, Guelph, Ontario.

"Martin R Ford does an extraordinary job with this book. I read every book on trees that I can find, and I found this book Why Trees? How to Love Trees both an education and an inspiration. He succeeds on every level in painting a story that not only answers the question, "Why Trees?" but explains why all of us need to love them. And for those of us who are already in love with trees, to not only love them more but to jump on the bandwagon of tree-advocacy. After all, trees cannot advocate for themselves. Clearly Mr. Ford has done this: he lives and breathes the miracle of trees. If you are not a believer in this miracle, all you have to do to become a convert is to devote the time and effort required to read this book.

A generation ago, my father Len Cullen, a career gardener, said to me, "A home without a tree is the reflection of an empty soul". This may sound harsh in the hurly burly strut of the day. We are often too busy to see trees.

However, viewed through the lens of this book, a lack of appreciation for the miracle of trees after reading it would make my father's words ring true."

Mark Cullen
President, Trees For Life www.treesforlife.ca

"Martin Ford's Why Trees? makes a compelling case for the mental and physical health benefits of trees in cities. Martin explains how trees play a vital role in improving life in our communities and why investing in tree health pays big dividends in healthy air, reduced crime, and climate adaptation. Caring for trees builds caring communities."

Mike Schreiner
MPP for Guelph and leader of the Ontario Green Party

"Martin's book offers a captivating journey into the world of trees, presenting complex topics in a refreshingly approachable manner. A fascinating exploration of the interconnectedness between humans and trees, his insight and research examine the many diverse aspects of trees, including the financial benefits that healthy trees provide.

He also discusses the importance of root systems, often overlooked in city trees, and the significance they have for tree health and survival. Martin's ability to weave everyday observations with his personal experience backed by scientific knowledge makes this book a revealing read for all seeking to deepen their understanding of nature's marvels."

Pranita Sawant
Landscape Architect

"Why Trees? is written in a nice, conversational tone that's not difficult or dry to read. Yet it's educational and informative...I've learned about the interconnection of trees to so many things - architecture, mental and emotional health, municipal planning and design, environmental pollution, for example. It makes a convincing argument for integrating more trees in cities, and for planting them in a way that maximizes their long-term growth and survivability. And of course, it conveys the awe and wonderment of trees in the way that we humans can experience them...that's the part I've enjoyed the most. The subtleties of the experience, whether observing the processes trees are going through or simply being in their presence, isn't something I've thought of much, but reading sections of the book about their magic makes me nod in agreement and want to run to a forest!"

Janet Ngo
Writer

Acknowledgements

Thank you to my wife Judy for her hours of dedication to reviews, suggestions, and edits. Thank you also to Hari Stirbet for planting the seed to put my ideas into words for others. And finally, thanks to Friesen Press for their expertise in gathering together the details to turn my manuscript into a book.

Table of Contents

"Ancient trees are precious. There is little else on Earth that plays host to such a rich community of life within a single living organism."

— Sir David Attenborough

"When we plant a tree, we are doing what we can to make our planet a more wholesome and happier dwelling-place for those who come after us if not for ourselves."

— Oliver Wendell Holmes, writer and physician

Community—everyone benefits

Trees are a silent wonder. When we are near them, we recognize this sense of wonder as a common bond with each person who gazes at them and sighs inwardly in pleasure—a shared smile that says what words cannot. It is the awakening of openness that enables community to form around and with trees.

We stop and want to speak about what we see and feel, so we look for words and feelings we don't normally acknowledge, such as peacefulness and calm. When these emotions are felt, they enable each of us to enjoy the presence of others nearby. We can then take the risk of connection, when normally we would walk on. When we meet again in the future, the experience of the trees' gift becomes an unquestioning and everlasting re-awakening of a shared bond.

We would have abandoned the idea of having trees in our cityscape if we enjoyed seeing only buildings and roads, but as humans, we knew we wanted trees to be a part of our community. We could have built all over the parks and open spaces and not planted trees on or along our streets, not included them in our gardens—simply visited them out in the national parks away from cities. But we didn't!

Instead, we tried to grow them amongst our buildings and roads. Unfortunately, we didn't prioritize what they needed most, which was healthy root systems. We didn't know that the roots needed to breathe, or that there were even such essential organisms in the soil as mycorrhizae which, when present, aid the roots to survive in limited soil masses.

We knew trees needed water, but we thought it was more important to have hard surfaces around the trunks for pedestrians; we conveniently assumed the tree would somehow find water. Some amazingly do manage to send roots deep enough to reach the water table—if the water table hasn't been drained.

We want trees in our cities—that's not disputed. It is how to give them what they need to firstly survive, and then to thrive, that has become the learning curve.

We want trees because of the pleasure they bring as well as their many other benefits. In understanding the skills of growing trees so that they thrive, we can begin to see that those same skills echo the skills of nurturing and caring for a human. Trees contribute so much to our neighbourhoods (while also cleaning the environment), and this encourages the caring that builds community.

Trees are a real solution to human-created problems, and we are learning to thank them for their gifts. Community is a word which we know as being "home" in a city experience—similar to the feeling we have with nearby extended family. We relax when we see familiar physical features that tell us this is where we live. When that place has trees, particularly large trees, then we easily recognize how deeply we (and others before us) care for this place.

"A tree stands strong not by its fruits or branches, but by the depth of its roots."

— Anthony Liccione, poet and writer

"A tree has roots in the soil yet reaches to the sky. It tells us that in order to aspire, we need to be grounded and that no matter how high we go it is from our roots that we draw sustenance."

— Wangari Maathai, Nobel Peace Prize laureate

"A tree without roots is just a piece of wood."

— Marco Pierre White, TV celebrity chef

Roots—the foundation of life

That the word "root" has been given the dual purpose of honouring our human origins and describing an essential part of a plant emphasizes how humans see roots as essential to the success of life in this world. We both originate from our roots—it is the health of those roots that enables humans and plants to thrive.

When roots emerge rapidly into favourable conditions, they explore and find other organisms to share and prosper with, leading to long and productive lives for the plant they support. The nurturing of these roots (by both nature and humans) is a skill above all others, because it is fundamental and therefore essential.

Just like humans, the roots of a plant need air, nutrients, and water. Trees live hundreds, even thousands of years, and so their root systems need to continually adapt to and explore the site they have seeded into. This is only possible if water and air exchange occurs continually throughout the soil mass they are growing in.

When we speak of human roots, we are talking about hundreds and thousands of years. However, as opposed to trees, humans have the ability to move from the place where they first put their roots down. As humans, we are not dependent on one site for nutrients, water, and air. Instead these commodities are imported—especially into the cities we have created and populated. Food is transported to us, water is either piped in from another location or wells are drilled, and winds usher in fresh air. We have devised roots outside of the soil. Trees do not have this luxury…

Yet they do have the ability to live many human lifetimes.

A tree planted in the city remains in the same place throughout its life. Yet we expect it to thrive, and its roots to continually adapt to its circumstances, regardless of what those may be. The hard surfaces which cover most of a city's surface area divert water away and seal off air from circulating in and out of the soil. Yes, compaction enables the hard surfaces and buildings to remain stable, but physically it stops root exploration and starves a tree of its basic needs.

Even if the soil mass humans have provided has enough nutrients, the plant cannot access them if it is unable to breathe and absorb water. And so, the tree may live for a while, but dies after a shortened life because its roots have been denied what they need to survive and thrive.

We have known, for some time now, that half of the trees we plant in cities die by their twentieth year after planting, and most of the surviving trees live just one quarter of their normal life span. These tree losses are almost solely due to our refusal to recognize the reality that roots need regular air exchange and accessible water to live—just as humans do. We know the problems and we have the solutions.

Now is the time to act.

If we think of the needs of a tree's roots as the same as what human roots need—clean air, water, and food—then we can learn to be attentive in giving city trees what they need to thrive.

"Trees are poems that the earth writes upon the sky."

— Khalil Gibran, author of *The Prophet*

"We can learn a lot from the forests, regrowth, change, and beauty."

— Catherine Pulsifer, poet

Seasonality—there are more than four seasons

Seasons "spring" to life through the trees around us. As the buds emerge, or later, as the leaves change colour and then fall, so a tree's presence in our lives dramatically tells us that the year is moving through the changes we call seasons. Other than snow falling, nothing in our city experience of nature is more visually dramatic than spring cherry bloom followed by leaf emergence, or autumn's blaze of colour and leaf fall. Both seasonal displays are seen as celebrations of life, and it is the tree's stature upon which these performances occur, magnifying our sense of awe and wonder.

When the canopy is full of leaves, we see the day's progression of the sun overhead through dappled light—the sunlight that has been able to avoid being collected by foliage. In autumn, when the leaves have gathered on the ground to be shuffled through, we are drawn with amazement to the limbs reaching upward and away from the trunk in arcs and curves.

A cityscape is dominated by fixed, human-built structures which rarely change, other than through a fresh coat of paint—it is as it was built. It can be beautiful, but does not offer more. Trees, by contrast, often produce flower and sometimes fruits or nuts. Both of these signal reproduction is occurring, another form of seasonality—the time to begin initiating new life during an existing lifetime. It signals that the tree has reached maturity and has the resources to create firstly the blooms and then the seed.

Each new season lasts anywhere from a few weeks (for the flower) up to five months (when a nut is ready to fall to the ground). Then the tree begins to initiate the bud formation for the next cycle. As humans, we notice these changes—we look forward to the pleasure of once again observing and peering into the tree's world, this tree that nature has included in our city lives.

"When the last tree is cut, the last fish is caught, and the last river is polluted; when to breathe the air is sickening, you will realize, too late, that wealth is not in bank accounts and that you can't eat money."

— Alanis Obomsawin, Indigenous filmmaker

"It is not so much for its beauty that the forest makes a claim upon men's hearts, as for that subtle something, that quality of air, that emanation from old trees, that so wonderfully changes and renews a weary spirit."

— Robert Louis Stevenson,
author of *Treasure Island* and *Kidnapped*

Pollution Control—trees are the easiest solution to our global crisis

It is in our cities where we create the greatest pollution. So, naturally, to be able to mitigate it at its source would maximize the benefits for those living in cities—and anywhere else on the planet.

Other than turning off cars and shutting down industry, the most effective and least costly solution to pollution is to have healthy trees filtering our air, cooling our roads and buildings, recharging our water tables, generating health-giving chemicals, reducing crime, and bringing us closer to nature.

Many of these benefits are not news to us—so what has held us back from treeing our cities?

There are cities famous for being treed, such as Vienna in Austria, which has well over forty percent tree cover. But this is only possible because the Viennese value trees and integrate them into their city life. Many cities are aiming for forty percent tree cover, but most hover around twenty-five percent or less. The principal reason this failure occurs is the death rate (fifty percent within twenty years of planting) amongst newly planted trees, which is disillusioning and costly.

There are several principal reasons why newly planted trees die so frequently: compaction, transportation, insufficient water, and drowning. These reasons are all theoretically understood but not addressed in practice.

Additionally, some new understanding shows that roots release carbon dioxide, and if this gas is prevented from escaping out of the soil (such as happens with compaction and hard surfaces), it prevents root growth. Not having open soil surface areas or other mechanisms for carbon dioxide to exit means the tree will not thrive, and in fact will slowly die.

Each of these problems has an easy solution if we recognize that when we plant a tree, the health of its roots is our primary responsibility. To address that, the long-term health of the soil we provide to trees must become our focus. That ultimately prescribes the skills we must practice, not just for the trees' sake, but so that we can tackle our pollution problem with healthy trees that provide us with clean air.

Planting millions of trees outside of the city in open areas sounds impressive, and is important, but it doesn't deal with the problem at its source. For example, consider cities where major polluters like factories are located. Here, at the point of origin, pollutants could be removed by urban trees before they ever made their way to areas outside of those cities.

It is empowering for populations living in cities to feel they can effectively help to recover from being part of the cause of our planet's health crisis. However, urban dwellers want to plant trees that live and prosper, and not simply place them in the ground with the hope that they will survive, as currently happens. A dying and unhealthy tree becomes part of the problem, instead of being the solution that was promised upon its planting. It no longer reduces pollution, and its removal and replacement only adds more to the city's carbon footprint.

Understanding how roots grow, and what soil needs to be healthy so it can support a healthy tree, enables each person to care for the trees they plant and to watch them mature and thrive, and thereby help to mitigate pollution.

"No tree has branches so foolish as to fight amongst themselves."

— Nigerian proverb

"Finland is officially the world's happiest country. It is also 75 per cent forest. I believe these facts are related."

— Matt Haig, journalist and author

Reduced Crime—without calling the police

Why is it that study after study shows crime in cities drops ten percent or more for every ten percent increase in tree canopy within a neighbourhood?

This phenomenon leads to extensive financial savings for a community, including a highly significant reduction in the costs of policing and the lengthy prosecution process. All of these benefits happen simply because of the presence of healthy trees, regardless of socioeconomic factors! This change is a permanent one, as long as the trees remain healthy.

When we add to this the health and social benefits arising from peaceful neighbuorhoods, it seems inarguable that planting trees should become the primary focus of every city—if only because of the massive cost benefits. The mystery, then, is why this knowledge hasn't permeated the population and administration of every city.

The cost savings and health benefits are real—so why the lack of action and follow through?

Unfortunately, trees are not seen as a priority even with these known benefits. Trees are seen as an extra, not essential. We haven't shifted our knowledge base yet to build these deeply significant advantages into our designing of city spaces, or to incorporate this understanding of what is beneficial and healthy for people. The resistance to this way of thinking is based on centuries of momentum which sees trees as an aesthetic choice and not as primary to the wellbeing of city life.

Trees that were planted twenty years ago are now mature trees, offering a plethora of benefits like health and healing, crime and pollution reduction, and improved stormwater management.

As the old Chinese saying goes, "The best time to plant a tree was twenty years ago…the second-best time is now."

"A tree that is unbending is easily broken."

— Lao Tzu, author of *Tao Te Ching*

"I took a walk in the woods and came out taller than the trees."

— Henry David Thoreau,
naturalist, author, and philosopher

Flexibility—trees are natural yogis

When big winds rush across our cityscapes, we see pictures of fallen trees with their roots pulled out of the ground. How often do we notice how small these roots systems are compared to the size of the canopy and trunk of a mature tree? It has become normal to assume the root mass will be small—after all, with a building on one side, two driveways on the either side, and a road nearby, we recognize there is not much room for those roots.

Of course they stayed small—they had no choice.

An urban tree grows, over the course of its life, to deal with average wind speeds. The leverage of the wind on its canopy is dealt with by the trunk flexing and absorbing the force of the wind. However, when winds are sudden or twisting, the force is quickly transferred down to the roots. In the small amount of ground anchoring a city tree, this results in the roots being torn out of the ground, as we often see on news reports following a storm.

It has been known for a long time that the worst thing to crash a car into is a tree, because it literally doesn't shift—or at least, its trunk doesn't. That's because the root flare at the base of a tree is designed to transfer forces from the vertical to the horizontal. The roots form a circular mass, embedded in stable soil, which absorbs movement through flexible grains of soil that are stacked together. The trunk of the tree stays perfectly still, while underground, hidden to the human eye, movement happens.

Even when we are not aware of it, nature is inherently flexible. Both humans and trees are living entities which adapt to their circumstances. Humans can change their circumstances and move on or rebuild. Trees stay within the site their roots grow into (or die, if the site is impossible, such as beside concrete foundations).

Soil is an example of that flexibility: water can pass into and through it, as can air and other gases.

This site flexibility is essential for us to provide when we are planting trees. Roots do not require much from us once they have explored the available space for them to grow into. Our job is to recognize, before we plant a tree, what it is that the roots need and how to provide them with the necessary underground (and above ground) root-friendly conditions. We must also be sure water is available in their early lives throughout the growing season, until the deep roots have found their way down to the water table, even if it is very deep.

Have a look at Stockholm's solution for city trees in Björn Embrén's YouTube video "The Stockholm Solution—an integrated approach to trees and infrastructure in the urban realm" and Pocket Woodlands' solution for city trees at https://www.pocketwoodlands.ca/.

Both of these examples show that when we first and foremost recognize and then meet the needs of the roots of trees, we are planting and growing trees in our cities to become a forever pleasure.

"We will be known forever by the tracks we leave."

— Dakota proverb

"The creation of a thousand forests is in one acorn."

— Ralph Waldo Emerson, philosopher and writer

Succession—timelessness and massive cost savings

Every young tree we plant is a gift to nature. It is one of the few real ways we can connect our cities to the original life on this planet, in a time before we created all the hard spaces and buildings which now house human existence.

The beauty of tree-planting is that the story of life doesn't stop with that first tree we plant. As the tree matures, it creates other young trees nearby, ready to begin rapid growth as the older tree slows down or is affected by disease. Mature trees provide homes for many other life forms, too, each of which provides its own benefits for the common ecosystem. Together, the continuation of the system becomes normal and self-generating—to be watched and enjoyed within our city experience…an ecosystem with a vision beyond a hundred years!

Humans have not forgotten the pleasure of a connection to nature—it is intrinsic to us—but it has been overlaid by priorities such as industrialization, academic scholarship, wealth generation, and sometimes war. Each of these is particular to the human experience and is not seen in nature. Nature is always in balance or moving toward balance, even though there may be events that cause stress, such as forest fires or drought. Adjustments may also be needed (for example, through attrition by disease) to address overpopulation.

When we plant a tree, we know it will live beyond our time; we know that the tree or its progeny can live for hundreds of years and be there for generations after us. Succession is both past, present, and future. When a plant germinates, it draws on past knowledge from within the seed and the soil. Once the plant establishes, it gives us succession in the present. And when it matures and produces fruit, it is providing succession for the future. All three of these—past, present, and future—are essential for succession to be fully realized.

Adjustments are succession's way of rebalancing when one life form has become the principal player amongst the many potential life forms that are always evolving.

The COVID-19 virus reminded us of nature's adaptability, and we primarily controlled its spread by refocusing human activity. Similarly, we can reforest our cities by refocusing human priorities. We need to recognize the benefits trees provide to humanity, and how, when we understand succession, we can start to see the health and life of trees as part of our own path to a healthy life within cities, and globally.

The trees in a desert oasis have become a succession only because water is available to them in an aquifer below the surface. The conifer, willow, and birch trees living near the Arctic, on almost barren rocky soils, live century after century (succession) because of a symbiotic relationship between the roots and the mycorrhizae that gather all the available nutrients and water into one accessible place.

Mycorrhizae is an interwoven network of fungi and plant roots within soil that have a mutually beneficial relationship. The fungi benefit by taking sugar from the roots of a plant (sugar is produced by the leaves of a plant and transported to its roots). The roots benefit by absorbing nutrients and moisture that is collected by the fungi. This web of mycorrhizae in the soil, consisting of fungi and roots, extends the overall surface area of a root system and greatly enhances the health of a plant.

Succession seen in the Amazon, where the soil is very poor, generally supports a myriad of life forms because of these symbiotic relationships in the soil. The classic evening rains of a tropical forest are collected and held by the mat of organic matter (including mycorrhizae) in the root mass. As a result, hundreds of gallons of water are available for the trees to uptake and transpire (exhale as water vapor) through their leaves into the atmosphere.

This transpiration is a cooling mechanism in a hot climate that would otherwise be barren. Succession has prevented the Amazon from becoming a desert like the Sahara, which could happen if we let its forest be destroyed.

There are examples of succession in each climatic region. These show us how, in cities, we can create an urban forest that is self-generating—another word for succession.

"From a small seed, a mighty trunk may grow."

— Aeschylus, Greek playwright

"If we lose the forests, we lose our only teachers."

— Bill Mollison, researcher and biologist

Adaptation to Circumstance—from bonsai to redwood

Adapting to the home we are born into… Imagine being a human who could not move after our first roots connected us to the soil we stood on. What would it be like if this was to be our home for hundreds of years to come, and the only place where we could find our sustenance and pleasure?

During the early years we would become aware of all that was around us. Our genetics would tell us that we had the potential to live a very long life. But for this to happen, we would need to focus on our young roots finding water. We would have to trust that our genetics, part of our parental gift, could enable us to adapt to climate change and determine our times of growth and our times of dormancy. And then our roots would discover fungi in the soil which would gently enter our new roots and form a network offering us nutrients and water. In return, we would give them the sugars created by our new leaves.

This newfound exchange makes available a whole new world of sustenance for the young tree, as well as an existing network of communication that connects it to other trees and lifeforms living in the soil. Now it recognizes that it is not alone like it once was as a seed. Instead, the tree is a living part of an evolving ecosystem with many possibilities and answers to difficult questions such as diseases, drought, and climate shifts. It taps into the world of experience and knowledge surrounding it.

But what if that seed finds itself on the side of a cliff? While its roots are able to anchor, life is difficult—yet not impossible. Water is only sometimes available, winds can be fierce, nutrients are hard to come by, sunlight is abundant but there is little shade, and the rock is hard. Though it takes time to explore all the crevices and cracks, its roots continue to explore and grow. There are others living on this slope, so life is possible, and there are mycorrhizae too, but their life is also difficult, and so they are small compared to the parent trees.

In this case the tree adapts and grows for a short time each season—as a bonsai does. Of course, a bonsai is created by humans continually pruning the roots, so the tree becomes used to limited growth. It is the tree's ability to respond to consistent but limited resources which means it will adapt and only grow slowly, even though its potential is to be large. When the tree has adjusted to this reality, it actually lives much longer than it would under its normal growing conditions.

Why growing slowly means they have far longer lives is still to be understood, but what is important is that they can adapt to a very tough growing scenario and have a more than full lifetime.

"We make an immense mistake when we think of trees as solely an aesthetic member of a community. They cut pollution, they cool the air, they prevent erosion, they muffle sound, they produce oxygen. Then, after all that, they look good."

— Dr. Richard Leakey, conservationist, and politician

"The cost savings produced by our urban forests make it clear that keeping the green on our streets, keeps the green in our wallets."

— TD Economics

Cost Savings—we all want that

The city where I live estimates the cost of planting a tree at four hundred dollars each. It is this number that we focus on when we think of the expense of planting city trees—this and the cost of watering during its early years. Yet if a tree prospers (and the numbers say it is a big if), it will create benefits and savings for the community for hundreds of years.

That is the number we need to pay attention to.

The many physical and emotional health benefits of trees have only recently been quantified, and those numbers are now beginning to be integrated into our costings so they can be of benefit to all city dwellers. When we include all the benefits and advantages of trees, that $400 initial cost shrinks into obscurity.

Here are the benefits that we know as of 2023. Some of them we are still putting a financial value/number to, mostly because it is difficult to quantify financial benefits such as mental health and the return of nature to our city experience.

- Cleaning both our air and water.
- Managing storm water, including erosion control.
- Slowing winds and increasing rainfall.
- Cooling our hard surfaces and providing much needed shade.
- Providing homes for birds and much of nature.
- Giving us an 11 percent drop in criminal activity for every 10 percent increase in tree cover (huge and immediate savings!).
- Providing health-giving chemicals and other indirect yet known health benefits such as better and faster recovery for a

patient whose hospital room looks out onto nearby trees (or a single tree).

- Calming traffic and providing safety for pedestrians.
- Creating a sense of community through the presence of healthy trees that live hundreds of years.
- Increasing the value of a home and/or district by a minimum of 10 percent.

And more...

If we take an example of applying even an annual one-hundred-dollar financial benefit per tree for each of the first nine benefits listed above, that means each tree provides nine hundred dollars' worth of benefit to residents of a city. And they do that for hundreds of years for an initial investment of less than four hundred dollars.

To any economist or investor, that's a no brainer!

"Knowing trees, I understand the meaning of patience."

— Hal Borlan, New York Times writer

"The forest is a place of peace and serenity, where we can escape the chaos and noise of modern life and find the calm and stillness within. It is a place of sanctuary, where we can find refuge from the stresses of the world."

— Unknown

Serenity—Om...

It is amazing that trees have the ability to live in such unwelcoming conditions, like on the side of a road.

Trees are amazing in so many ways. They can live longer than many human lifetimes. They are the largest life forms living in our city communities. And they ask very little of us other than to let their roots find what they need to live a healthy existence.

"Life is fundamentally active. Even in seemingly stationary organisms like trees, there is furious activity occurring at the microscopic level" (National Geographic April 4, 2022). Although we can't physically see that activity, we can appreciate the inherent wisdom in a tree's ability to coordinate all this activity to manifest the living entity before us.

Such appreciation and amazement evokes within us a sense of wonder. This wonder causes us to step out of our present work and family priorities and recognize a connection—even though we can't name it. As this happens, so too a sense of calm naturally accompanies our sense of wonder and leads to serenity—the acceptance of the world around us and our part in it.

As with meditation, words are put aside, removed from the forefront of our "now" experience. Our sense of wonder is enabled in the presence of a tree, or group of trees, to be beyond the words we use in daily life. It is the conversations of daily life that obstruct us from recognizing and accepting, whilst in a tree's presence, that we are actually in the present moment and feeling serene.

Serenity is a rare experience, yet the presence of trees gives us an easy opportunity to become familiar with the unfamiliar. Sadly, there are few opportunities to experience this serenity and acceptance in the hardscape of a city.

"Even a small tree casts a big shadow."

— Cameroon proverb

"Big trees cast more shadow than fruit."

— German proverb

Shadow—the pleasing kind

The beauty of the shadows that trees cast is that they vary throughout the day, as well as with each season. As the sun moves through its overhead arc each day, the light that passes through the canopy shifts, continually creating visual variations which capture our attention, even when subtle.

Each sunrise or sunset is individual, depending on cloud formations, but what is important is that the light from each is low on the horizon. At that time we tend to see up into the tree, and thus see more clearly how high the tree reaches into the sky. This height effect is unique in our human lives because it's not coming from a building we created, but rather from a natural entity living with us in the city.

A building is typically unable to create shadow on the face of its own structure, and so any sense of depth is limited to recesses such as windows and entrances, or maybe the overhang of a roof. Even then, the lines of a building are typically straight, both vertically and horizontally. Straight lines we notice, but not for long.

Shadow from the canopy of a tree is three-dimensional. It shows both depth and height, as well as mass. When we see all three dimensions, we start to notice the details and intricacies of a tree's structure. This encourages us to stop and slow down, and we respond emotionally. We are drawn to its uniqueness.

Trees rely upon curves to provide both flexibility and strength. Nearly all trees have curved, arching limbs, a circular trunk, and a rounded canopy outline. A curve is a strong shape that is able to flex in variable winds as well as adjust to carry the load of an emerging leaf canopy. As a tree moves and sways in shifting winds, and the angle of the sun changes with the progression of the day, light filters through from different directions.

We can see shadows dancing in new patterns.

A tree's shadow creates the fourth dimension of time. One of the ways it does this is in our recognition that a tree has lived many years in this place where it first set its roots—it was here long before we entered into its presence. We often ask how old a tree is, even when it is young! We find it intriguing to try to put a number to its existence, even when it must be a guess, since we weren't there when the roots and shoots emerged.

When we do come up with a number, it is often an underestimation (especially as trees typically grow more slowly in a city scenario). If we find out the actual numbers, we are impressed to learn of its true age and wonder what the tree has seen over its many decades.

A story always fascinates our sense of wonder, and a tree is an amazing story.

"Trees are the pillars of life, holding up the heavens and anchoring the earth. They are a symbol of stability and security, reminding us that we are never alone in this world."

— Unknown

"Suburbia is where the developer bulldozes out the trees, then names the streets after them."

— Bill Vaughan, journalist

Engineering—our understanding revolutionized

The largest structures we built up until two hundred years ago were amazing, vaulted cathedrals. These buildings required heavy outer structures to hold the inner high ceilings in place—buttresses, which even some trees in tropical forests use to stabilize themselves. Then, in the late 1880s in Barcelona, Spain, an inspiring designer named Gaudi (who enjoyed nature all through his childhood) recognized the importance of flexibility. This is the reason we can build such tall buildings today.

This quote is from Wikipedia (https://en.wikipedia.org/wiki/Antoni_Gaudí): "Gaudi conceived the interior of the church as if it were a forest, with a set of tree-like columns divided into various branches to support a structure of intertwined hyperboloid vaults. He inclined the columns so they could better resist the perpendicular pressure on their section. He also gave them a double turn helicoidal shape (right turn and left turn), as in the branches and trunks of trees. This created a structure that is now known as fractal. Together with a modulation of the space that divides it into small, independent, and self-supporting modules, it creates a structure that perfectly supports the mechanical traction forces without need for buttresses, as required by the neo-Gothic style. Gaudi thus achieved a rational, structured and perfectly logical solution, creating at the same time a new architectural style that was original, simple, practical and aesthetic."

Gaudi saw what had been in front of us all along, but was not recognized for the brilliance of its engineering because it was only part of nature: the tall and flexible trunks of trees.

He asked the question, "How can a tree reach such heights on such a narrow column, and then spread a canopy so wide, yet also be able to flex when the winds come from different directions?" He then summed up this understanding with the statement, "There is no better structure than the trunk of a tree or the skeleton of a human."

A tree's structural priority is to have the flexibility needed for its roots to remain undisturbed in the same soil mass over the many centuries it expects to live. The human skeleton's priority is to have the flexibility to roam over the planet's different surfaces; for that we require the body to adapt rapidly—a different type of flexibility such that our lifetimes can only be one century.

As Gaudi said, both the tree and skeleton are equally amazing in their ability to absorb stress, but each has a very different priority— each has properties which have changed how we design today and in the future. Both come from nature's ability to adapt, and every adaptation is a result of nature having so many potential "solutions".

As Einstein is quoted as saying, "We still do not know one thousandth of a percent of what nature has revealed to us." He also said, "Look deep into nature, and then you will understand everything better." Or to paraphrase: if you want to understand a question, you must look to nature—clues to the answer are already there.

"The tree is a chemical factory."

— Diana Beresford-Kroeger,
medical biochemist and botanist

"There is a growing body of research that shows exposure to trees provides positive health benefits. More specifically, research demonstrates that walking in a forest can decrease symptoms of anxiety and depression, increase vigor, decrease cortisol levels, and increase our ability to recover from stress."

— Tree Canada

Healthy Chemicals in the Air—improved health without Big Pharma

Why is it that both the Japanese and Korean people have recognized Forest Bathing as being healthy for its people, and include this understanding in their cultural values?

Their lifespan expectations are six years longer, on average, than the U.S. numbers and without the need for medication. Of course, that difference is not all due to the health benefits of trees; there are other factors at play. Still, it is clear that trees play some role in achieving a long, healthy life.

We don't fully understand how being amongst trees is a factor in these health differences, but several factors are known. Firstly, being around trees brings about a reduction in stress levels. Secondly, phytoncides released by trees into the air we breathe are known to benefit our health.

Phytoncides are a plant's defense chemicals against bacteria and fungi. When we breathe them in, they encourage our white blood cell production, particularly the NK cells (which are specialized in hunting cancer cells). This increase gives our bodies improved means to deal with tumors and viruses—vital for our health. This benefit is simply gained from walking in a forest or living in close proximity to healthy trees, particularly conifers.

Why conifers? They give off higher concentrations of phytoncides, and their needles do this all year long.

A third factor is that there are locally higher levels of oxygen around trees compared with the levels in a city setting. This is because of the release of oxygen from leaves when sugars are broken down, and because the canopy helps to keep the oxygen concentration beneath the leaves, instead of it floating off into the atmosphere. Oxygen is important to all life forms.

We now know that when a healthy tree is being attacked by an infection or insect, it has the ability to almost immediately recognize the identity of the attacker and make specific defense chemicals to create a particular response—very similar to what our immune system does for us. Amazing as it is that these chemicals are so quickly created, what is also important is that they are released not only for self-protection, but also to inform other trees. An attacked tree releases airborne markers, so other nearby trees can recognize the threat and anticipate the problem by increasing their production and release of chemicals ahead of an infection or insect presence.

This ability to share information is one of the advantages of planting trees in groups rather than as single isolated specimens (as is typically seen along streets and in gardens). Interestingly, city trees, which are often under stress, create specific, beneficial chemicals that help them cope with the stress of their growing conditions. These chemicals also benefit our health and reduce our stress levels but unfortunately the benefits come at the expense of trees that struggle and are aesthetically unappealing. To recognize trees as significant givers of health will reduce both our healthcare costs and our reliance on solutions provided through pharmacare. A walk in the forest or sitting under a tree in your backyard or park has both preventative and healing benefits for city dwellers worldwide; it is a cure like no other.

"Someone is sitting in the shade today because someone planted a tree a long time ago."

— Warren Buffett, businessman and philanthropist

"The older the tree, the more shade it provides."

— Romanian proverb

Shade—who doesn't like a bit of shade on a hot day

We love to be outside when possible, and trees enable that to be a year-round experience in any geographical location—especially when the canopy of multiple trees meet.

In warm weather, the coolness we experience below a canopy is partially due to the sunlight being absorbed by the leaves. The canopy immediately absorbs the direct rays of the sun and cools our skin while protecting it from ultraviolet rays. However, we also experience coolness because the leaves transpire water brought up from the soil to cool themselves. In the tropics, a tree may transpire as much as 800 litres in a day. This process of changing water from liquid to gas requires energy, just as happens in our refrigerator's cooling system. For trees, that energy is withdrawn from the surrounding air (latent heat factor).

We know now that the temperature advantage is amplified when a group of canopies in a city extend for an area one acre or more in size. The impact is cumulative because the air is often stabilized (winds are slowed), enabling the cooler air to naturally fall to the ground for us to enjoy. In the past, when the larger spreading canopies of the elm tree dominated our northern streetscapes and created an almost continuous canopy, we actually had a cooler city experience.

Flickering light is a silent pleasure, but when it is accompanied by winds, the movement is magnified. We notice the movement and hear the stir of leaves—a gentle sound, but one that causes us to look up and notice. A canopy also gives a home a sense of privacy, even when it is a tall specimen. The tree is a pleasure to look at, and so we don't see the houses beyond—we focus on what we want to see!

Each of these pleasures are without financial cost, and shared with those who pass by and notice. And we have the advantage that our bodies are not being stressed by exposure to direct sunlight.

Additional economic benefits from shade occur when the roofs of our houses do not transfer the baking sun's heat into the house. Air conditioning, which has become the greatest peak demand on North American power systems, is reduced, particularly if the shade is from the south during the height of the midday sun. As well, when our streets have a tree canopy arching above the roads, hard surfaces of concrete and asphalt do not heat up as much. When no canopy exists, open and exposed road surfaces retain the sun's heat even after the sun goes down (known as the "heat island effect").

Sun exposure is a major cause of skin cancer. Trees block or diminish the ultraviolet rays so that we don't have to stay indoors or be sure to apply as much sunscreen. And most importantly, we can let our children play outside under the leaves and not worry so much about their young skin.

Trees enable us to connect to the outdoors like no other faculty—it is one of the many gifts they give us without question. They only ask for a drink of water to continue giving us their gift for centuries to come.

"A tree provides shade to all."

— Kenyan proverb

"Only by planting trees, we will be able to overcome global warming."

— Vivek, actor, environmental activist

"The net cooling effect of a young healthy tree is equivalent to ten room-size air conditioners operating twenty hours a day."

— USDA Forest Service

Cooling—more important now than ever before

Trees are the cheapest air conditioners that a city can run—and they are a benefit to everyone, not just those who can afford to buy a mechanical air conditioner. Importantly, it is a continuous cooling that the trees' leaves provide naturally; this cooling is available throughout the day, unplugged from the power grid!

This side-benefit of trees is of particular significance to the elderly population, whose bodies do not regulate internal temperatures as easily. They also have thinner skin, which is a lot more vulnerable to ultraviolet light; they can safely sit under a tree, but without shade they would need to be indoors with air conditioning turned on.

Another bonus is that trees are the least polluting air cooler available—they actually remove pollution. This is done without cost to the city, since they don't draw on the power grid. All these benefits are free and available at times of peak need during the height of summer. So why aren't healthy trees, along with all the benefits they bring, our first priority when designing city spaces?

As our cities have spread over large areas of countryside, roads and roofs have replaced previously green surfaces and their heat moderating effects. The dark, hard surfaces of roads (particularly asphalt) coupled with exposed roofs of houses in direct sunlight increase heat retention.

If tree canopy were the priority in city design, areas of exposed hard surfaces would be significantly reduced, and we would benefit from free cooling. These effects last hundreds of years, with few maintenance costs aside from supplying water to the roots during the heat of summer (which minimizes stress on root systems and enables the tree to continue growing and extending its canopy, which in turn creates further cooling effects).

Healthy root systems and a water supply are all that trees ask of us. And so, we are back to the question, "Why aren't trees the first priority in our design of cities?"

"A tree gets water from deep within."

— Kenyan proverb

"Until you dig a hole, you plant a tree, you water it and make it survive, you haven't done a thing. You are just talking."

— Wangari Maathai, environmental activist,
Greenbelt Movement founder,
and Nobel Peace Prize laureate

Water Retention—soil gets thirsty, too

In cities, hard surfaces and grading plans, which are primarily designed to cope with exceptional one hundred-year downpours, divert rainwater away from entering the soil. In effect, most of the rain which lands on a city is redirected into storm sewers or onto 'molded' land shapes. This naturally available water, which would normally replenish the soil, quickly ends up in rivers and heads out to the sea or lake.

In suburban areas, hard surfaces are estimated at forty percent or more coverage. That number climbs to as much as eighty percent in the intensity of cities' downtowns. This adds to the problem of low water tables. It is one of the principal reasons that even in existing wooded areas, which are saved as part of an urban plan, trees will slowly die unless they are near a water source such as a river or lake.

Simply, urban roots are deprived of ground water and can't adapt to the drop in the pre-existing water table.

The opposite can also be true—tree roots drown (one of the biggest killers of young, newly-planted trees) due to local soil compaction. This causes water to sit and saturate the soil surrounding the root ball without being able to drain away, thus drowning the tree.

One of the primary functions of soil and subsoil is the ability to hold water in a consistently available manner over a tree's growing season. Most importantly, it does so in amounts which don't displace the soil's essential ability to aerate the roots and mycorrhizae in the soil. Organic matter, and an organic material called biochar, are the means for water to be held in a sponge-like form around soil particles.

These mediums allow plants to draw on water yet allow excess water to slowly drain down to the water table.

When our construction techniques prioritize how to give tree roots a healthy existence, then at the same time we create systems which replenish the soil and the water table. This significantly reduces surface water runoff, which in turn reduces the infrastructure costs of designing a city and the cost of watering trees and replacing them every twenty years or less.

A number which may seem shocking, but not surprising, is that a 10 percent increase in the organic matter content of soil means it holds 20,000 more gallons of water in every acre of land. And because organic matter creates soil which is open in structure, rainwater is able to move deeply into the soil rather than becoming runoff. This both recharges the local water table and reduces the need for stormwater management construction—very important savings to a city budget.

Plants desire a consistent supply of water, as do all life forms, but trees in particular have the potential to grow deep root systems which then create the large-canopied trees that cities want and need.

"Climb a tree to see the world."

— Unknown

"Children who play under the trees are nourished by nature."

— Lailah Gifty Akita, inspirational writer

Places to Climb—the child in all of us

A child's desire to climb a tree is their way of understanding their exciting body's ability to explore its potential—and then to be able to view the world from another perspective. The child's mind sees the tree and wants to be among its limbs, to pull themselves through the various levels until they can reach no more. Then, they like to sit and recognize what they have achieved, without anyone else's help, simply because they wanted to ask the question, "Can I do this?"

A tree is not a man-made structure like a playground—it is both original and living. The child is aware that the tree has been there long before they came into this world, and it will be there for centuries to come.

When a child scales the limbs of a tree, it feels like a friendly place—a place to return to when there is a need to be oneself. It is a place where they do not have to discuss or respond to anyone other than the tree, and where they can feel the sense of wonder that being in nature brings in a simple and real way.

The dappled light passing through leaves fascinates our senses. Set a young baby in a cot so they can look up into the canopy above, and they will be absorbed by the play of light. When we are older, we remember our child-self's fascination and want to lay again and simply watch the patterns that absorb both our visual and auditory senses with the rustle of winds passing above.

A tree is a quiet gift to a child, and so easily given.

"The tree is a shield against the wind."

— Kurdish proverb

"The wind whispers secrets to the trees, and they, in turn, share them with us."

— Indigenous American proverb

Slowing Winds—whoa Nelly!

Being under a tree as the winds move their limbs, particularly when it is in leaf, is a dramatic and extraordinary way of experiencing energy being passively absorbed. The canopy sways with the gusts but quickly returns to its original form—all the energy from the wind is transferred through the limbs, down the trunk, and through the root flare into the roots and beyond into the ground. All this, without the need for nails or concrete. And if, on another day, the wind comes from a different direction, then it will be absorbed from that direction also.

However, this ability of a tree is dependent on its roots being extensively grown into the soil. It needs a large, stable root ball in order to transfer energy from its canopy down through to the anchoring soil mass to counteract the power of the winds.

If a tree has only a small amount of soil to live in between the hard spaces of road and house or sidewalk, its roots have nowhere to grow into because they are surrounded by compacted soil. Furthermore, the tree is too isolated to benefit from the intermingling of other tree root systems as it would in a group or line of trees. As a result, an individual tree is much more vulnerable to strong winds.

It is the ability of roots to share a soil mass which results in groupings of trees being much better able to resist the force of winds. In effect, the overlapping root systems are like a textile which shares the sideways (or sometimes downward) motion of the wind over the connections between each tree.

In other words, all the trees would have to fall before one alone could succumb to the wind's force.

This gives us yet another essential reason to plant trees closely together along streets, and preferably in groups. Groupings of tree canopies mean that an individual tree is part of a larger upper canopy surface that both deflects and absorbs winds thanks to their shared surface area. It allows the most flexible part of trees, the leaves and smaller branches, to respond quickly and thus effectively absorb the energy of a gust.

This slowing and deflection of wind has multiple advantages for trees living in cities—and for the humans living near them. One benefit is that moisture evaporation from the soil is reduced, which helps prevent roots from drying out. Another benefit is that rain is slowed as it falls through the leaf canopy, minimizing run-off and erosion. This is also a particularly effective way to replenish our soil during rainstorms in the dryness of summer.

Yet another benefit is that the need or pressure municipalities feel to design large expensive stormwater management systems is eased. And because land surface under trees is cooler, it will not fuel the storm by adding more heat from the land. The canopy and the coolness of the land absorb the energy of both heat and wind and steadily, passively, and effectively reduce the energy release of a weather system.

And then there is the joy of hearing the rustling of leaves from a gentle wind. This sound masks the sounds of a city and gives us the sense of pleasure that being amongst nature brings—the joy of connection.

"The tree is known by its fruit."

— Saint Basil the Great, Archbishop of Caesarea

"The earth laughs in flowers."

— Ralph Waldo Emerson, philosopher and writer

Flower and Fruit—a bounty for all our senses

In spring we anticipate, are amazed by, and celebrate the blaze of colour from cherry and magnolia flowers. We know that the fruits and nuts (avocados, cherries, oranges, apples, almonds and many more) which develop from a tree's flower are some of the most nutritious and health-giving foods our bodies can enjoy. And even if the flowers or fruits are not something humans eat, then the bees gather pollen and nectar while birds and animals enjoy the berries and nuts, enabling a natural ecology to return to our streets and gardens.

And we watch with fascination, especially if we have a bird feeder to encourage year-round "fly-bys."

We have zoos, parks, and arboretums for the most unusual organisms in nature, but these are museums for specimens that come from the nature outside our cities. We make the time to visit these places so as to have an idea of nature's wonders, and therefore its possibilities. But while such places can inspire us to be more creative in our city spaces (as can a well-run plant nursery), usually we see only their ornamental benefits, and not the systems in which these life forms co-exist.

Recently, after the crisis facing our bee populations, we began creating pollinator plantings as a garden design form, and planted more trees in open, empty areas within our cities. However, planting trees which produce fruit, pods, and nuts is still unwelcome—usually the term "messy" is used to avoid including such potential food and pleasure sources. There has even been a movement to plant only male trees (masculinization), which we know from the human dynamic is always a disaster!

Having flowering trees brings seasonal and unique joy as we watch with wonder the emerging colours in petals, the bees arriving, and then the birds flocking to enjoy the eventual fruit harvest. These pleasures are framed by the upright structure of a tree; we need only look up into its branches—we don't have to go anywhere—and the gift is there in our gardens and streets.

Knowing the flowers come first, we can then await with anticipation the bees' arrival, then the fruits' enlargement, and hopefully also colour and scent appeal. As the fruit ripens, so too do the seeds inside. These seeds are the succession that enables nature to create new plants, naturally programmed (I prefer the word "potentialled") to grow very deep root systems and begin their path into maturity. They do all this without any cost or maintenance requirements from us—they have nature's perfect root system, which can adapt to city conditions quickly.

We must learn to trust nature. As Einstein said, "Joy in looking and comprehending is nature's most beautiful gift."

"Biochar works so extremely well for the trees."

— Bjorn Embren, Swedish Tree Officer

"Biochar can be used to address some of the most urgent environmental problems of our time—soil degradation, food insecurity, water pollution from agrichemicals, and climate change."

— Dr. Johannes Lehmann, Cornell University

Biochar—a gift to soil that lasts for centuries

Biochar is the product of a 1000-year-old method of taking organic matter and baking it at 450°C without oxygen, creating a stable form of carbon which lasts many hundreds of years in soil. Its structure becomes a home for nutrients and water as well as beneficial soil organisms.

Its physical structure aids the drainage and air exchange that soil needs, and it can absorb both carbon dioxide and methane, making them available for plants to create sugars and carbohydrates. The list of its many beneficial uses, including acting as a carbon sink, has led to it being called "black gold."

With our focus on trees in cities, the best example of the benefits of biochar for city trees is seen in the Stockholm Solution, which uses biochar as its primary "soil" medium for tree roots to grow into.

In the year 2000, Björn Embrén, a Tree Officer for the City of Stockholm, was given the task of saving the city's dying trees. In 2015, he presented his findings and methodologies, which revealed remarkable success in growing very healthy city trees. This methodology is now mandated for all city tree planting in Sweden. And in 2019, he showed how a biochar and compost mix has become fundamental to their tree-planting system, once again with tremendous success.

Both presentations can be found on YouTube and are applicable world-wide, as they meet both the engineers' requirements and the needs of plant roots.

"The best mulch works just the way fallen leaves and branches do in nature to protect and enrich the soil naturally."

— Davey Tree

"Mulch is the ultimate multi-tasker in the garden."

— Unknown

Mulch—why it is so important

Mulch gives a tidy appearance around trees (but not up against their trunks!) and is a visual pleasure, but that is not the most important reason for its presence in cityscapes. The key reasons why mulch is so important are cooling of the soil, inhibiting weed competition, encouraging mycorrhiza growth, reducing soil compaction, maintaining soil moisture, aiding erosion control, enabling human access under trees (without compacting the soil), and discouraging physical damage to young trees.

All of these reasons are deeply important for enabling trees to survive and thrive.

Mulch helps us to recognize and distinguish a space as being for trees. When that happens, we act more considerately than if the tree is surrounded by hard surface or grass. A serious problem for young trees is when bikes are tied around their vulnerable bark, leading to physical damage that kills the tree. This happens far less frequently when trees have mulch surrounding them, especially if they are placed on areas of raised soil.

When we notice mulch is an organic material, it reminds us that recycled wood fibre and bark are a symbol of what happens in a forest—that the material from dead trees and leaves will normally remain on the surface and eventually become soil as they decompose. This adds another connection to nature's way, and provides a welcome relief from the isolated feelings we have when our surroundings are dominated by concrete and asphalt.

We have a new sense of what is possible for life inside a city—our creativity is expanded.

"A tree is a wonderful living organism which gives shelter, food, warmth, and protection to all living things. It even gives shade to those who wield an axe to cut it down."

— Buddha

"Acts of creation are ordinarily reserved for gods and poets, but humbler folk may circumvent this restriction if they know how. To plant a pine, for example, one need be neither god nor poet; one need only own a shovel."

— Aldo Leopold, conservationist and ecologist

"Whoever has learned how to listen to trees no longer wants to be a tree. He wants to be nothing except what he is. That is home. That is happiness."

— Herman Hesse, author of *Siddhartha*,
Nobel Literature Prize laureate

Home in the City—welcoming our new neighbours

Natural systems enable cities to survive. We rely upon clean air, sewage handling, storm water issues, and more for urban living. We are also dependent on each of these for our well-being and health.

We tend to believe that we can manage our city environment to create healthy conditions, but it involves expensive energy use and massive infrastructure costs. Each of these infrastructures are coping mechanisms that need huge financial investments to continually provide essential maintenance and upgrading. Because their focus is on providing for human function, in the past these systems were designed by engineers and architects, whose training rarely includes an understanding of nature's ability to augment these systems.

When we create engineered systems using nature, we enhance the human experience of living in a city so that it is a pleasure to live in, rather than an experience to be endured.

We are coming to understand that including nature's needs in all our decisions is essential. Within that paradigm, how to grow city trees successfully has been one of our most difficult tasks. When we have healthy, successful tree canopies in our cities, we value our city experiences more. And so too do all the other living systems of nature who adapt to life in the city and find a home amongst the trees.

It is the root system of trees which is essential for us to focus on in order to 'grow' city homes for both nature and humans.

When we have healthy trees, and especially when their canopies meet to form a continuous living ecosystem, then the rest of nature recognizes we have made the decision to include them in our human landscapes. They may not yet feel welcome, but they do see an opportunity to live with us—much the same as cats and dogs do when we bring them home.

We love our pets and give them a lot of our time and resources. The same should be true of a landscape we value, as it too gives us continual pleasure when it is healthy. Our pets are our connection to nature, but so is the tree on our street or near our home. When we freely give such care and loving attention to our pets, why is it that we do not do the same for our trees outside, making sure they get all the resources they need, even if it is only water to be able to survive dry times?

We know how to grow trees and what they need to establish. If we think of nature as essential to our well-being, then we will give trees the means to be healthy. And once their roots are thriving, they will grow for hundreds of years, giving joy and all the other benefits of trees to generations of city dwellers.

"Though a tree grows ever so high, the falling leaves return to its roots."

— Malawian proverb

"Information is like compost; it does no good unless you spread it around."

— Eliot Colemanorganic, farmer
and agricultural researcher

Compost—feeding the new with the old

Composted organics is the human name for the process of creating food for the mycorrhizae which are essential in building the health of a soil. There is a tendency to think of compost piles as a way to store and break down fallen leaves, pulled weeds and left-over organics from the kitchen. In other words, its value is seen in being primarily for disposal within the city scenario, rather than being a natural part of nature's richest by-product for the healthy soils we all benefit from.

In modern times, though, we are ever more cognizant of what constitutes soil health. Because of the importance of replenishing soil, we now must wonder where we will get all the organic matter that we need to feed all of our soil, especially as we recognize that applying fertilizers has a damaging effect on the balance within a soil, and that its overuse eventually silences natural systems. When that happens, we end up growing plants hydroponically or in pots and boxes.

These are very expensive alternatives which have limited long-term benefits; they are containers filled with artificial soil designed for attractive plant appearance and quick sale.

Compost can also be a mulch when applied to the surface of a plant bed. As a mulch, it inhibits weeds, though it is mainly ornamental. Usually it is a lovely, dark colour—we humans recognize dark soil as healthy because we inherently know that there is organic matter and moisture present, and therefore it is a good growing medium.

Every part of a plant can be returned to the soil, where soil systems "digest" and make use of each and every part. Nothing is lost when compost is our focus—especially when the heat generated by decomposition is able to build up and oxygen is available. This rapidly speeds up the decomposition process. Then not only do we readily provide food to the soil, but we keep its systems active and resilient, and this enables roots to thrive and explore—happy trees!

"The soil is the great connector of lives, the source and destination of all."

— Wendell Berry, environmental activist and novelist

"Treat the Earth well: it was not given to you by your parents; it was loaned to you by your children."

— Indigenous American proverb

Soil—getting the dirt

Soil is a mystery to us, but as we learn to observe it, it awakens in us a sense of wonder. It is the health giver—constantly living and evolving, full of creatures such as worms and microorganisms, it stores masses of water, carbon, and nutrients, and gives us both health and food.

The question for humanity becomes…other than air and water, what is more important than soil?

Why do we think of it as being something to be used rather than the treasure that it is? A treasure which has taken thousands of years to become a balanced home for roots of plants to grow in and with. And when the plants' season is over, their fallen mass replenishes the soil by feeding soil organisms with their composting leaves, stems, flowers, and roots.

Soil is a balanced structure which adapts to climate, seasons, mineral availability, drainage, and erosion. It can be very deep, for example in the prairies or old peat bogs, or it can be a skin of organic matter matted on top of a rock or unfriendly geological deposit. Either way, it is still soil as far as a plant is concerned—a home in which the plant can anchor its roots and obtain the nutrients it needs.

We name this organic/mineral layer "soil" when it can grow plants. Soil is essential to our existence as humans—we are dependent on this organic matter. Humans have become the dominant living form on Earth because we learned to use soil to produce a predictable source of food, and we felled forests to build the homes we live in.

We call this planet "Earth" (another name for soil!) because it is the part of the surface from which we collect our harvests. But for soil to be considered healthy enough to grow crops, it must have an open physical structure so that air and water can both enter and leave the soil. Wet or compacted soil cannot be used for growing plants, and roots will barely survive for any length of time, if at all, when the soil has been harmed by machinery or robbed of the organic matter needed to feed the soil organisms that create a healthy open structure.

This leads us to one of the principal reasons why half of the trees we plant in cities die by their twentieth year, even after being set into a city landscape that has been "designed"—because it is designed without prioritizing the health of the soil and subsoils that the trees' roots are expected to grow into.

In urban settings, trees' need for healthy soil has not been prioritized, because we did not recognize just how essential healthy soil is for tree health. The question becomes…how is it that this happened and continues to happen? Why is it that tree health has not been understood as being dependent upon root health and that root health is dependent upon soil health and water availability?

Why did we miss the obvious?

"In the end, we will conserve only what we love. We will love only what we understand. We will understand only what we are taught."

— Baba Dioum, Senegalese ecologist, environmentalist, and forestry engineer

"A nation that destroys its soils destroys itself."

— Franklin D. Roosevelt, former United States president

Erosion Control—ground control to Major Tom

Trees are the most effective and inexpensive solution for soil erosion. There is nothing better than a mat of healthy roots and mycorrhizae to bind the particles of soil in place when there is a lot of water or rain impacting an area.

They do this by literally connecting the independent soil particles, both horizontally and vertically. This three-dimensional equivalent of a fabric-like structure allows water to pass through gently. When the soil has reached its saturation point, additional water is diverted to the surface, where it continues its journey downhill, slowly moving over the roots near the surface.

Most importantly, the soil mass itself remains intact. This would not be the case if the interwoven mesh of a healthy root system did not exist.

Additionally, the canopies of trees, particularly if they meet or are close together, dramatically slow the progress of rain as it falls through the leaves and branches. This stops the physical impact that a downpour of rainwater can have in breaking the soil away from the roots that hold it together. The slowing of water arriving on the soil's surface is particularly important in times of drought, so that the soil becomes damp first and is then able to absorb the much-needed water, instead of it running away from the plants to a lower point.

A canopy also reduces the desiccation of understory plants by shielding them from strong sunlight. When rain enters a cooler soil mass, it is less prone to evaporation and able to do its job of recharging the water table. In effect, the tree's canopy, the understory plants, a cool soil mass, and a healthy and adaptive root and soil microorganism community provide a deep filter system so that water is retained and thus the soil mass is also stabilized.

For humans to build such an effective erosion control system would be hugely expensive and involve engineering that we haven't even thought of yet. That is because nature is a living entity and adapts to changes in circumstance. It does this especially effectively when most of the original tree cover is left in place, a tree cover that has been adapting for millennia to maintain the biosystem it is part of. Natural succession systems rapidly replace lost trees and so maintain soil stability.

In city scenarios, the trees which are growing must adapt to their environment before they can help with erosion control. They can only do this when they have a healthy start and their root systems can explore deeply. We can offer them this healthy start by planting in a way that enables this to happen so that they live their full potential lifetime.

This then kickstarts a biosystem that will have all the beneficial erosion control abilities of a healthy woodland. And it is so inexpensive compared to engineered so-called solutions!

"Roads were made for journeys, not destinations."

— Confucius, Chinese philosopher

"A tree never hits an automobile except in self-defense."

— Woody Allen, film maker and actor

Traffic Calming—so we all get home safely

Highways are designed for the purpose of moving vehicles, but the humans inside those vehicles are ignored and treated as automatons, disconnected from the surroundings they are passing through. Of course the journey becomes something the driver wants to get over and done with as quickly as possible—hence road rage and falling asleep at the wheel!

When vegetation is included in highway design—for example, highways that are divided between each direction, with trees growing along both sides—then the need to simply complete the journey is moderated by the pleasantness of the scenery. Nature and the countryside are a real reminder of life beyond our busy work lives.

When we design city streets with trees as a priority, the overshadowing canopy cools the road surfaces and provides dappled light which has an immediate calming effect upon our behaviour and response. In years past, we would plant a single type of tree to create a metaphor for each street. In modern times, many different species would be included because we recognize that diseases, which are a normal part of nature's cycles, must not be able to devastate a monocrop canopy (as happened with the elms and ashes). These varied streetscapes also interest us visually and slow both traffic and pedestrian movement.

Speaking of pedestrians, when we closely plant groups of trees in sidewalks and walkways, they encourage us to slow down instead of rushing, an added benefit to shopkeepers. This works very effectively for downtown shops along sidewalks, as these groups of trees, when planted on raised planting beds, have the effect of being small woodlands. Their canopies become a place to rest under, especially when seating of some form is included around the edge of the growing area, particularly for older people to shelter from both the sun and rain but also for children.

When we include children's play in these woodland designs, by placing mulch over the soil surface, we create another reason for families to wander around and be part of the downtown. Our malls are places to shop, but downtown generally has a more interesting history and mature trees, especially groupings of trees, which are landmarks and add greatly to the feeling that this is home.

"Autumn paints in colors that summer has never seen."

— Unknown

"Colours are the poetry of nature."

— Unknown

Colour—the joy of rainbows and oh, so many greens

Greens are colours known for calming and healing—and calm is a gift to our health and our sense of well-being. Under a tree's canopy the light is filtered into patterns, and the greens become many shades which shift as the sun arcs through its day. If there is a breeze, it adds to the continual reshaping of the shadow's patterns. The older leaves of a tree, which are lower in the canopy, have to be able to capture a lower level of light and so are often darker than those newer leaves. As we look up, our eyes see dark progressing to light and create three-dimensional depth which is emphasized by the limbs holding up their distant canopy.

Recognizing the scale of this structure creates a framework in which the colours can be appreciated—a living work of art.

If there are flowers, dramatic colours are offered seasonally. Once pollination is completed, they drop to the ground as petals to be enjoyed as a carpet over lawn or walking surfaces. The flowers (such as cherry and magnolia blossom) are a transformation greatly anticipated each season.

And then comes autumn, when the leaves fall as the tree prepares for the coming cold season (or, in tropical climates, some trees defoliate seasonally for several weeks for health reasons). The autumn colours of these leaves are yellows and reds or simply brown, but they are dramatic in the effect they have on our cityscapes.

Children love to play amongst these leaves, and adults shuffle their feet and listen to the crunchy, rustling sound—so different from the sound of walking on hard surfaces that is normally heard when they pass along sidewalks.

The sky's blues and greys are a lovely backdrop for the greens of the canopy set against it. This is particularly true with conifer trees, which generally have a very vertical form but also a darker green to their canopy. This darker green contrasts noticeably and reminds us of all the variations of nature.

And then there are those trees we have classically selected for their colour specifically, such as Japanese maples, which hold their reds, oranges, and yellows from spring until autumn. We have chosen them for colour and they offer that pleasure each time we see them.

"The feel of rough sun-warmed bark of an ancient forest giant, or the cool, smooth skin of a young and eager sapling, gave me a strange, intuitive sense of the sap as it was sucked up by unseen roots and drawn up to the very tips of the branches, high overhead."

— Jane Goodall, anthropologist

"The bark of a tree is its autobiography."

— Richard Powers, novelist

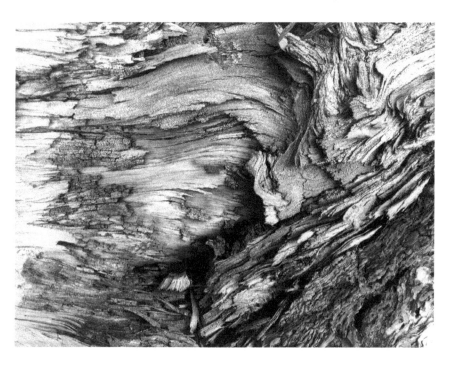

Bark—and not from a dog

The London plane tree has been admired for its dappled bark since the hybrid was first discovered 300 years ago. It became a dominant species to plant in cityscapes because of the visual effect of its unique bark—and because being a hybrid meant it was a particularly hardy tree in city conditions.

One of its parents was the North American sycamore, which has a similarly mottled, characteristic bark (and while its bark is not as strongly defined, it is still striking). Climatically, the sycamore is a lot hardier than its hybrid progeny, but we are so drawn to the colours and textures that barks offer that we focus on the London plane's bark features, instead of the hardiness of its parent sycamore—a far more important skill for surviving in today's cities around the world.

Another beautiful bark is that of the birch tree. The bark can be white or red, and interestingly peels off over time, revealing other colours beneath. It has a cousin, the aspen, that is not often planted (even though it is a lot tougher tree than the birch once it is established), likely because its white bark isn't as strongly coloured.

So colour is one aspect that barks offer, but most of the trees we see have bark which is lumpy, with variations of brown in colour. The primary role of bark is to protect the thin "skin" of cambium below, which are the living cells of the tree that transport water up to the canopy and sap down to the roots. Bark has an additional role, one of preventing water and sap loss from the transportation tubes, as it has basically a corklike texture and is therefore impermeable.

Because bark is not a living structure, it is also difficult for pests and diseases to pass through it to the functioning cambium cells. That is why some trees have very thick bark—it keeps the internal structures cool and protected. These thicker barks are visually interesting. They feel very old, which in fact they are, as the depth of the fissures show the "stretch marks" from the tree's expanding diameter.

With a mature tree's leaves being so high in the canopy, it can be difficult to identify the species based on leaves. Some barks are very distinctive, such as beech and eucalyptus. For others, it is possible to narrow down the potential identification of the species by becoming familiar with bark formations. This adds to our connection with the trees we are passing.

When we think of bark as having the function of skin in protecting the living material beneath it, we recognize that it is similar to our own skin's function, and how it too becomes gnarly with age. The wrinkles of human skin are often attributed to the wisdom of age and so too, do we think of older trees as having "seen" so much. We appreciate the wisdom they have to offer—they have survived, and often show their healed scars where bark has grown over damage or lost limbs.

"Never say there is nothing beautiful in the world anymore. There is always something to make you wonder in the shape of a tree, the trembling of a leaf."

— Albert Schweitzer, humanitarian and physician

"For in the true nature of things, if we rightly consider, every green tree is far more glorious than if it were made of gold and silver."

— Martin Luther, theologian

"Trees are complicated, fascinating things, usually older and more beautiful than any of us."

— Monty Don, horticulturist and broadcaster

Wonder and Amazement— every moment of the day

All of life's many forms amaze us, yet when we see a huge living entity like a tree, we are left in wonder—especially when it is living just down the road.

That feeling of wonder has the effect of "grounding" us in the present moment, while at the same time connecting us to the natural world in ways that normally only Richard Attenborough can do. What distinguishes trees from the other parts of nature we see each day is that they don't move around—they are a constant presence. And when we add the knowledge that they have lived, and will continue to live, hundreds of years in that same soil, then we recognize this place is their forever home.

Once again, our realization leaves us in wonder—how?

Each season, the trees transform our landscape as they respond to the approaching change. In spring, we are fascinated and wait with anticipation for the new leaves to emerge from the buds which formed last year, and have waited through the winter to "spring" into growth. Why do they choose this time, when it is still cold? Sometimes they even start emergence and stop. How and why do they decide to wait?

Autumn is the opposite, as the leaves sever themselves from their parent, after much of the cell content is withdrawn to be stored in other parts of the tree—an amazing skill! Conifers choose to hold onto their needle leaves, and somehow manage to keep water moving to the needles, so they don't dry out over the long winters. And come spring, the older needles are dropped, having helped the tree survive the fluctuations of both temperature and available moisture. How is all this possible?!

Like humans, each plant is unique. Each has its own story of adaptation to its home environment or conditions. The White cedar of North America (Thuja plicata occidentalis), for instance, is a tree that likes wetland conditions, but can also live with less water, and generally lives several hundred years. And yet, on the side of the Niagara escarpment in Canada, that same species has found a home on bare rock face and has been shown to be over 1200 years old.

All those years ago, the seeds which happened to lodge and then germinate in a crack in the limestone recognized that their home was a difficult one, and that they could only expect to grow slowly—very slowly. The White cedar, being an evergreen tree, needed to find water for its leaves and roots all year round, or it would dry out in the wind and sun. Early in its life it recognized the limits of its scenario and adapted to the home it found itself born into.

How? We are left in wonder and awe at how it added 1000 years to its lifetime.

"At first I thought I was fighting to save rubber trees, then I thought I was fighting to save the Amazon rainforest. Now I realize I am fighting for humanity."

— Chico Mendes, Brazilian labour leader
and environmental activist

"Raindrops are not the ones who bring the storm but the trees that stand taller and dance in the rain."

— Unknown

Increasing Rainfall—who would have guessed

The canopies of trees slow the speed of passing winds. This reduces evaporation from the soil and gives the air a greater capacity to hold moisture. The clouds are not rushed away, but instead pause and add their cooling effect by blocking the sun.

As the clouds warm up throughout the day, they are more likely to release rain, as we see each evening or late afternoon in a tropical climate. In the Amazon, as the rainforest is being destroyed and cut down (killed), rainfall is decreasing.

Each day in a hot climate, mature trees need to cool their upper leaves. They do this by evaporating water, drawn up from the soil, through their leaves (transpiration). This recycling of water into the atmosphere accumulates over the day and forms the late afternoon rains, which return the water to the soil to be lifted the next day through the tree's roots, into its trunk, and up into the canopy where it is needed. And so the land and the plants remain cool and well-watered. This recycled water supply is provided by the presence of trees. The Amazon, without trees, would be one more desert.

Our cities can often be deserts as far as trees are concerned!

"Wood is universally beautiful to man. It is the most humanly intimate of all materials."

— Frank Lloyd Wright, architect

"Wood is nature's own artwork, waiting to be shaped and brought to life by skilled hands."

— Unknown

Timber!—the most flexible of natural building materials

At the end of a tree's life, we are left with the gift of a durable and malleable material that we can shape and be creative with. This material, wood, is continually replenished—unlike the oil and gases which we make plastics from, or the steel which requires huge amounts of energy to smelt and form.

Living trees build their fibres into a light but very flexible structure without an expensive manufacturing process. That is why wood is still the predominant material for building housing, if there is sufficient available.

The other qualifier is climate—where there is a more humid climate, wood doesn't last as long and so harder materials are favoured for the walls, but it is still used in roof structures.

Wood is also a medium for art; it can be turned into furniture or flooring, showing off its grains and growth rings that tell us the unique story each piece of wood has. We know that when we see something made of wood, its value changes because it is from nature and it is individual, like a sculpture.

Wood has a "feel" to it, which steel or concrete rarely have. When wood is planed to a smooth surface, it has a gentle quality, one that feels warm and welcoming. It can even be stained to suggest another impression. Whatever the use, what we create from the trunk of a tree will last hundreds of years.

And let us not forget it also had a life as a living tree which gave us pleasure as it grew amongst the family of trees it began life with, whether part of a forest or a streetscape somewhere. So many gifts.

"In a forest of a hundred thousand trees, no two leaves are alike. And no two journeys along the same path are alike."

— Paulo Coelho, Brazilian novelist,
author of *The Alchemist*

"A forest is a symphony of trees, each playing its own part in the grand composition of life."

— Unknown

Variety—open 24/7

Every tree is unique, and there are so many species to choose from. Some have flowers (magnolia) and fruit (mango) or nuts (walnut), some are smaller (dogwood) and others are huge (tulip tree), some like shade (ironwood) or semi-shade (redbud) while others love direct sun (Guanacaste), some have coloured leaves (like the red of the Japanese maple) and others have unusual leaf forms (mulberry).

Some live fifty years (poplar) and others live 1000 years (oak), some love damp soils (elm) and others love near-desert conditions (palm), some hold their leaves all year (evergreen) while others drop them for six days or six months before growing them again (deciduous). Some have narrow crowns (fir) and others have one hundred-foot wide crowns (ceiba), some grow buttress roots twenty feet tall (kapok) while others have almost no root flair at all (pear), some have taproots which dive one hundred feet into the ground (Ficus), and others have mostly a surface root spread (beech).

Mangroves actually live in water, while palms live around a desert oasis. Some trees have thin bark, often with many colours (eucalyptus), while others have deeply gnarled and corky bark (pine). Some trees (aspen) spread by underground roots which push shoots to the surface to become another tree or trees, yet they are the same plant growing over hundreds of acres.

Some woods are very hard (ebony) and others are very soft (balsa). Some trees grow very fast (willow) and others grow slowly like the burr oak.

There are so many potentials to choose from and to be enjoyed—the plant kingdom is something we taste in our lifetime, but rarely do we immerse ourselves in its wonder. The choices for living with trees in our gardens abound, and their presence gives us much to observe and wonder about, and learn from.

"To be without trees would, in the most literal way, to be without our roots."

— Richard Mabey, writer

"The Mother Trees we think of as the big, old trees…they catch your eye when you walk into a forest."

— Suzanne Simard, scientist

"The Mother Tree cradles the forest in her branches, offering shelter and sustenance to countless lives."

— Unknown

Mother Trees—they get my vote

Suzanne Simard, a hero to me and many others, coined the idea of a Mother Tree to fulfill the observation Darwin first introduced to us—that plants adapt, and that adaption is based upon the available surrounding resources and the tree's genetic potential. Mother Trees are the oldest and usually largest trees in a forest or woodland. They are the ones with the most experience in adapting to problems such as pests, disease, and climate fluctuations.

They also have extensive root systems that are amplified by the mycorrhizal population within the soil.

Suzanne's work was inspired by her childhood growing up in a forest. She had an inkling that there was something wonderful happening in the soil, which her young mind thought of as being caused by fairies. At that time, there wasn't another word available to explain what she "knew." The symbiosis she introduced to the world came to her after working in the replanting system of Canada's forestry industry and recognizing that what she witnessed was not creating a healthy forest.

She returned to university, where she began showing how trees of different species traded nutrients and water.

This didn't go down well with the scientific establishment, because although it was inarguable that there was an exchange going on, it was considered unacceptable to suggest that it was being done consciously, and without a central decision-making processor such as a brain. How could that be?

What is important about Suzanne's work is that, although we may not yet know how nature communicates and makes decisions, we know it is happening, as she showed us. Nature has been functioning this way long before humanoids evolved. The question that arises is, "What is intelligence?" and "How is it communicated?" ...To be continued!

"There is a necessary wisdom in the give-and-take of nature—its quiet agreements and search for balance."

— Suzanne Simard, scientist

"A tree's strength lies not only in its roots but also in the symbiotic alliances it forms with the world around it."

— Unknown

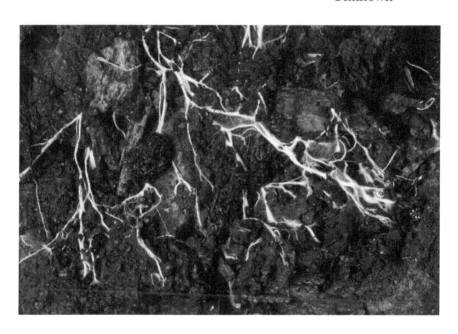

Symbiosis—unravelling the mystery

Symbiosis, which we generally understand as being the sharing and exchange of resources between organisms for mutual benefit, is often difficult to achieve in the soil we provide for city trees to live in. This soil typically has insufficient aeration and is nutrient-poor and lacking in organic matter, thereby inhibiting the potential for symbiotic growth of healthy bacteria, mycorrhizal networks, and tree roots.

Although people living in cities reap so many benefits from trees, we often give trees little to help them to live healthy and full lives. When we plant trees, it is frequently into a pit in the ground that has been engineered to remove water, and the soil has been compacted to support solid structures. The trees are rarely watered and often damaged by machinery or human activity, such as bicycles or foot traffic over their root systems.

Their leaves are also swept away rather than left to recharge the soil as they would in a forest, and so the soil around the roots degrades over time. A constant supply of organic matter (such as decomposing leaves) is essential for symbiosis to occur.

We plant trees singularly, when what they like most is to live in mutually supportive groupings where succession naturally occurs and the seedlings are able to take advantage of naturally deep root systems. They also begin life as nursery-grown transplants, whose root systems must recover from being miniaturized to reduce transplant shock, a known killer of young trees.

Although mycorrhiza can be added to soil during planting to reproduce the symbiotic relationship trees normally have with soil microorganisms, these organisms are unable to survive if the soil in which the tree is planted is compacted, water-logged, has little organic matter to process, or has mycorrhiza that is incompatible with the tree type.

Symbiosis is fundamental to all life on Earth. When we understand this universal bond, we will choose to plant city trees in a way such that they will thrive. By supporting trees to thrive in the city we too will have a healthier and happier symbiotic life, as we will reap the many benefits trees provide to us.

"In the forest, we find peace, clarity, and purpose. It is a place of refuge from the chaos and noise of the world, where we can reconnect with ourselves and with the divine."

— Unknown

"Learn character from trees, values from roots, and change from leaves."

— Tasneem Hameed, writer and peace activist

Sanity—when surrounded by crazy

When they live near us, trees become a constant in our lives. We associate them with a sense of calm.

In city life, there is a need for calm. There are few opportunities to truly experience calm in the presence of another living entity… to feel acceptance and to appreciate positive things, with no words or explanation needed. When we see a healthy, long-lived tree, we are moved—we are in awe and admiration for the magnitude of its presence, strength, and skills to survive in diverse and difficult circumstances.

Sanity is health on multiple levels. It is peace of mind; it is how we accept our own very personal story in all the forms it takes and through all the events that make up our lives. When city and family life requires us to fulfill so many demands on our time, focus and care of "my own time" becomes scarce as well as unfamiliar. Our context becomes the story through which we live.

The presence of a tree, simply and without words or conversation, tells us there is another way of being. It offers a place beside its roots to be and to ground ourselves. Those recovering from post-traumatic stress (especially after war) find much of their understanding and acceptance during group time with others who have "been there," and are then encouraged to spend further recovery time with plants and animals, as this enables the individual's recovery to be integrated.

Being with nature and not having to use words or explanations helps us listen again to our innate sanity—the person we were before the tragedy. Animals and trees accept these survivors as they are, and so the recovery of their self continues. Sanity is an individual path, and we see a tree as shelter along our way.

"In the shelter of trees, rain becomes a gentle symphony, soothing the soul and nourishing the earth."

— Unknown

"During a storm you seek shelter under a tree and not the clouds."

— African proverb

Shelter—from the storm

When we think of trees, we often have a memory of sheltering from rain that is deflecting off a leafy canopy above. Or we think of sheltering underneath when big winds rush out of the sky, or the hot sun is baking down upon us as we step outside, or when air conditioning is too costly or unable to keep us cool. It is during these times that we relish sitting under the cooling shade of a large group of trees.

When we have bad news and need somewhere to sit so we can recognize how we are changed by this news, then trees are a contemplative place. When children want a place to be by themselves, they will climb into the limbs of a tree and watch the world below— and stay there for hours. It becomes one of the strongest pleasurable memories of childhood.

The storms in our lives come in many forms, and so trees, which we know live past many human generations, become symbols of the resources and realities beyond the present experience we are encountering. They can gently shelter us in our gardens and our streets at any time of day or night. Sometimes we look to them as our constant—they can even feel like a parent as they look down on us from above, and we sense that they are taking care of us!

Because, in fact, they do.

"Palm trees, conifers, and deciduous trees stand as living storytellers, each whispering tales of their respective habitats and the cycle of life."

— Unknown

"Try to forget what objects you have before you—a tree, a house, a field, or whatever. Merely think, 'Here is a little square of blue, here an oblong of pink, here a streak of yellow,' and paint it just as it looks to you, the exact color and shape, until it gives you your own impression of the scene before you."

— Claude Monet, painter

Palms/Conifers/Deciduous— so many choices

Palms, conifers, and deciduous trees each have a very different outward appearance. Generally a palm is one long stem with a group of leaves at the top, a conifer is an evergreen, as is the palm, but with limbs attached to the sides of a central trunk covered in the leaves we call "needles", and a deciduous tree is similar in structure to an evergreen, but characterized by its ability to shed its leaves. This shedding occurs when the seasons change such as fall to winter, or alternatively for disease protection.

Each of these three types of trees become taller by extending the lead shoot. For a palm, if its lead shoot dies then that stem will die, even though they are very tough trees (although there may be regrowth from below). Both conifers and deciduous trees can regrow a secondary lead shoot if necessary, or redirect their shoots sideways to gather available sunlight.

Each of these three distinct and differently-shaped trees are part of the landscape potential of the world. Each of them has many species and varieties, with various colours and forms, as well as rates of growth and lifespan. They also have different root systems, which can need very specific conditions or be remarkably able to adapt to tough city conditions.

All of these variables mean that trees are a vast subject about which few people in our present industrial and academic world have the extent of knowledge and experience needed to be able to grow successfully, particularly in cities. Such knowledge is a lost art and a lost skill. This is changing, however, largely because of the new generation. Those of us who love trees are fascinated by them—the wisdom of trees and their capacity to help the planet. We want more trees in our lives and around our homes. We miss them.

"Trees, like wise souls, shed their old branches, allowing room for new growth and transformation."

— Unknown

"Self-pruning is the shedding of branches that are shaded or diseased, which are potentially a drain on the resources of the tree."

— Wikipedia

Pruning—did you know trees naturally self-prune?

Once a tree has set its roots into the place where it will live for the rest of its life, it recognizes its circumstances and adapts. It can also anticipate the future! If it is alone in a wide-open space, it will be able to easily find all the sunlight it needs and so will grow vertically for a short while before sending lateral shoots or branches sideways to create as wide a canopy as possible to maximize its leaf area.

If that same tree is surrounded by other trees who are growing at the same time, then each tree will still do both—grow vertically and produce side limbs. However, the tree is aware of the competition and knows that as it grows taller its lower limbs will be obscured from the light and will no longer be of value.

At the base of each limb, where it attaches to the trunk, is an abscission layer of meristematic cells which have a distinct function. These layers of cells are waiting for the time that the limb protruding from the trunk will abort and fall off. At that time, the meristematic cells begin their intended function of growing very rapidly to cover over the gap and thus prevent disease from entering the woody fibres which do not have defensive chemicals.

Basically, the meristematic cells re-establish the continuous skin over the tree's surface, which we call bark, and the tree then continues its plan to grow upward into the light. This is an amazing skill which shows the tree anticipates its future.

"To secure correct soil conditions, it is necessary to provide for each and every tree as follows: (1) a sufficient amount of good soil; (2) sufficient moisture; (3) proper drainage; (4) proper aeration of the soil; (5) a supply of plant food."

— D. Cox, researcher

Berms—trees love to grow on them

A berm is a raised soil mass of any shape and size. When we focus on root systems, the greatest advantage we can give newly planted trees and shrubs (and fortunately the easiest) is to plant them in raised soil. This enables air to easily and continually move in and out of the soil mass, while at the same time allowing free drainage around the roots.

Although on first impression it would seem that planting trees on berms and in raised beds would displace rain, the soil mass of a raised area of soil is open in structure and so water is absorbed readily. Even more importantly, the roots will spread quickly to the base of the berm to collect the water there as well.

With its height, a berm becomes a landscape feature as well as a healthy root-growing medium. Its vertical presence is of sufficient soil volume to be noticeably different from the landscape around it, particularly in the uniformity of cityscapes. A berm can have any soil volume and height desired. It is an all-season presence, however its benefit to plants is the primary reason to include it in landscape design.

Its potential as a landscape feature depends on how you wish to shape your space. A berm is a permanent yet adaptable presence in the landscape that can re-channel water movement and collect and allow rain to naturally recharge the soil mass. If a berm is two to three feet high, newly-planted trees on the berm will appear more mature, due to the additional height, than trees planted at grade with the surrounding land, an immediate benefit both financially and aesthetically. And they will grow to maturity more quickly because of the berm's favourable growing conditions. This increases the value of a new landscape and the sense of privacy from neighbours. Berms also invite children to play on the slopes and amongst the trees.

After a berm is built and planted up, cover the surface with a mulch of your choice. Not only is this attractive, but it is important for both stabilizing the soil surface and cooling the soil mass, which are particularly crucial for new roots emerging into soil. The soil mass of a berm will dry out much more slowly than a flat, compacted soil surface, as it can hold a larger volume water and so the need for watering is reduced. And when rain falls on mulch, it has a soft, porous landing, resulting in more efficient rainwater absorption.

The definition of a berm is variable, as it depends on the setting and function/s needed with each site. When building a berm, try putting stakes in the ground up to the height you would like to see the berm, and then add soil until a level is reached which feels comfortable—make each berm your own.

It is simply a shaped, raised mound of soil, but the benefits to our plants and landscape experience are extraordinary—especially given the minimal cost to create it.

"To exist as a nation, to prosper as a state, to live as a people, we must have trees."

— Theodore Roosevelt

"People who will not sustain trees will soon live in a world that will not sustain people."

— Bryce Nelson, journalist and professor

City trees—an invitation

Over the last century, we have come to acknowledge that animals are feeling beings, and so are deserving of our care. Thus, including pets in our lives, is an example of adding to city life in a way that makes it healthier and more enjoyable for humans.

Whether or not one believes that a tree is sentient or not, a tree is a living being. Trees in cities give multiple benefits to all city life and, as such, their value can be even greater than pets since every single person receives a measure of well-being from the trees' offered gifts.

A tree also elicits both emotional and physical responses from us, from our bodies and our minds—we feel connected to the living tree in front of us. And if it dies or struggles to live, we recognize the feeling of loss.

Trees do not move from where their roots first anchor them, and therefore do not require a central nervous system or organizing structure, such as a brain, which animals need to be able to migrate and explore. Yet trees live hundreds of years, responding to such changes as irregular seasons, drought, disease, erosion and winds, fire, competition and symbiotic relationships, variable reproductive cycles, and having their canopy eaten.

We are only beginning to discover the amazing capabilities found in nature and to include them in our understanding of a living being. Trees need very little of our help to prosper, but they do need us to provide soil and water for their roots—as well as the canopy and trunk care to enable a healthy and full lifespan. When we acknowledge a tree's living needs, and design our cities to include these needs, then we will have accepted that they are living beings who we can live and prosper within our city lives.

Why would we accept urban life without trees, when all that is needed is that we value their needs as being in parallel with human needs? In reality, it is a symbiotic relationship.

How to Do It—how to prevent early tree death and instead get all the benefits

Here are some final ideas and guidance on ways we can plant trees in our own home landscapes and community spaces to give us the vibrant and healthy urban trees we all love.

Succession as our present day "holy book"

What weight does the word succession carry that it has become our mantra? The significance of understanding succession is that it means we, as humans, can acknowledge nature's incredible skills—skills we are able to learn through watching what happens when we step back and listen.

Succession occurs automatically in nature, naturally. Nature is normally in balance through sharing with all other life forms, which is particularly important when there has been a major change such as a wildfire or climatic shift.

That isn't the case within cities, where the isolation of trees and parks by construction and hard surfaces inhibits living systems from sharing resources and chemical information, and further compromises the shade needed to moderate temperature fluctuations and water availability. Cities are unfriendly deserts to trees and nature. Succession and symbiosis are mutually dependent.

But they don't have to be.

When we create growing places for any form of plant, soil and roots need to be our first priorities. Next comes the recognition that nature is thousands of years old—it has a succession plan.

When we choose our plants, we can have the "now" trees to give us the size and visual pleasure that larger specimens grown in nurseries have. At the same time, we can consciously plant the next generation of very young trees and shrubs, which will benefit from growing in the shade of their adult companions and become the next generation.

These young plants will form a normal root system that will be far more self-sustaining and enable the full and normal lifespan that nature expects for them. Succession planting (planting seeds along with one- or two-year-old trees) is also very cost effective, as replanting will not be necessary and initial costs are minimal.

Most important is recognizing that shrubs and trees in nature enjoy living close together (one and a half metres, or five feet, is commonly seen in young woodlands). To replicate this, planting in groups is essential, and having both shrubs and trees together will give visual and seasonal pleasure, as well as a diverse ecosystem for the roots and soil organisms.

And crucially, amongst these planting groups of areas designated for woodlands and ornamental beds (not lawns), we must include tree seeds. This will ensure the presence of trees for the future because the root systems of seedlings, as they emerge into the soil, will naturally explore deeply. Deep root establishment enables trees to thrive (with minimal costs) and have a lifetime of hundreds of years. The planting of seeds completes our desire for a healthy succession that we pass on to the next generation so they too can enjoy all that nature offers.

How to plant trees in the city so their root systems are happy

There are five essential needs for roots and trees to be able to thrive:
- Aeration (both in and out of the soil mass).
- Consistent drainage.
- Consistent water sources from the upper surface.
- Young planting (trees planted within their first two years of life) so as to minimize root pruning during transplant
- The inclusion of multiple tree species.

There are five additional needs which will encourage deeper root system development of seed-grown plants:
- Deep soil mass (ensuring there is no compacted layer).
- Water at deeper layers in the soil.
- Specific/suitable mycorrhiza.
- The biochar needed to host them.
- Revisiting to sow more seeds if any of the first seeds didn't take.

Watering

It is essential in the early years that a tree is not stressed while its roots establish, especially if it is an older tree with a small root system that has been dependent on regular watering in the nursery. A shortage of water in these early years can put the tree into transplant shock, which can be fatal. If it does survive, it will have minimal root growth for that year.

Even after it is established, once it is unable to find water it will stop growing for that season, and usually cannot restart until the next season.

It is important to have soil which holds water in its structure so the new roots will explore the soil mass. It is essential that the soil has consistent water and air available to it, and that it is able to freely drain. It is an investment in having a healthy urban forest to be sure watering is included in the budget for newly planted trees—you would be surprised how often that is not the case!

How to create good growing conditions and taking care of the surface water

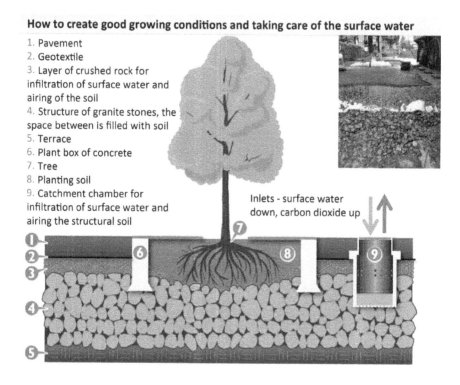

1. Pavement
2. Geotextile
3. Layer of crushed rock for infiltration of surface water and airing of the soil
4. Structure of granite stones, the space between is filled with soil
5. Terrace
6. Plant box of concrete
7. Tree
8. Planting soil
9. Catchment chamber for infiltration of surface water and airing the structural soil

Inlets - surface water down, carbon dioxide up

Image credit: Hildegun Nilsson Varhelyi, City of Stockholm, Sweden, presentation by BJörn Embrén and Britt-Marie Alvem.

Stockholm Solution for tree planting

A video from a September 2019 presentation shows the successful solution Sweden has integrated into their city tree planting program which focuses on root health. They satisfied the engineering needs for city construction by the use of large rock to meet compaction levels but with naturally occurring twenty-five to forty percent open spaces for root systems to explore. They also designed with both aeration and water recharge for the roots in mind—very well explained and very successful. It is now policy for tree planting for all of Sweden's city tree plans.

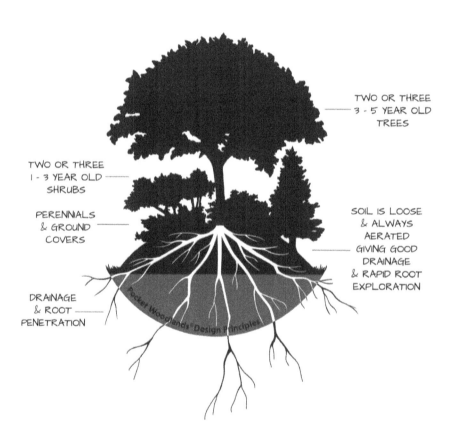

TWO OR THREE
3 - 5 YEAR OLD
TREES

TWO OR THREE
1 - 3 YEAR OLD
SHRUBS

PERENNIALS
& GROUND
COVERS

SOIL IS LOOSE
& ALWAYS
AERATED
GIVING GOOD
DRAINAGE
& RAPID ROOT
EXPLORATION

DRAINAGE
& ROOT
PENETRATION

Pocket Woodlands® Design Principles

Pocket Woodlands

There are five principles of a Pocket Woodlands design:
- Creating a raised planting area of an uncompacted soil mixed with organic matter.
- Planting a mix of young and older "now" trees to provide a landscape feature and succession.
- Setting the trees at no more than one and a half metres, or five feet, apart with shrubs amongst them.
- Adding a mulch layer to cover the surface attractively and to cool the soil mass.
- Ensuring that any compacted layer below the raised planting bed has been disturbed so as to allow water drainage and deep root growth.

Besides the health advantages of Pocket Woodlands, the raised planting bed is a three-dimensional landscape feature in a normally flat cityscape. It is inexpensive to build, it slows vehicles and pedestrians, and fixed engineering and services can be easily placed within the berm's design.

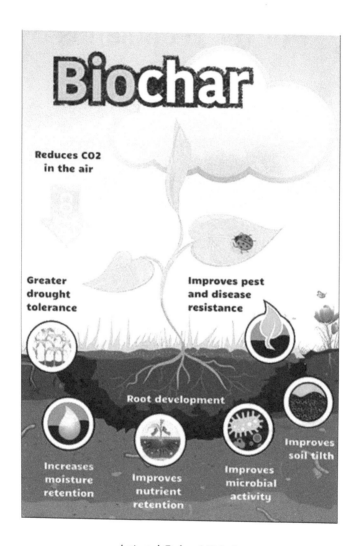

Activated Carbon NZ Ltd.

Soil/biochar

Watch the Stockholm Solution 2019 presentation on planting trees to see the soil ratios and the use of biochar/compost mixes which have been shown to create very healthy root systems for all plants.

Biochar is charcoal made from burning organic waste material without the presence of oxygen. It is used as a soil amendment to increase soil fertility and studies show it increases agricultural productivity. It has the potential to help mitigate climate change because of its ability to sequester carbon. When added to livestock feed it has been shown to aid digestion and reduce methane emissions. Biochar has become better known in recent years and is now widely available.

Biochar/compost mixed in with clear stone (no sand) provides the ability to hold water and nutrients, plus creates a healthy mycorrhizae home, which is both freely draining and retentive of all that the plant's root system needs. It is also very straightforward and easily created and placed by machine, thus avoiding compaction issues.

Drainage/water tables

Water is essential, and yet deadly if it is not able to pass through the soil and beyond the root system so the roots can breathe. If the water table is three meters (or more) below the soil surface, then this is sufficient soil depth for the upper mass of roots to be healthy.

When root systems find this water table, they will be able to draw water during times of drought when the upper feeding roots do not have water available around them.

Landform to capture water

Where possible, direct the runoff water to the soil mass so that it can replenish the water level, particularly during summer's dry times. See the Stockholm Solution and how they found many benefits as a result of directing the water collected from roads into the ground around the trees, rather than into a culvert system (very large savings as well).

As long as the soil freely percolates the runoff, then trees benefit greatly from any runoff water.

Salt

The normal application of road salt is not an issue if the soil system is healthy and freely drains. Previously, salt has been attributed as being the primary reason for the death of street trees in northern climates.

The importance of seed-grown root systems

A seed's genetics are initially focused on growing a deep and extensive root system. A young plant knows that it is the roots which will provide water and nutrients, create stability, and sustain the tree for its expected lifetime. But it also needs to understand the existing conditions and potentials in the soil and subsoil so that it can adapt its growth.

If water is scarce, the seed will prioritize growing a deep root system to search for a reliable source of water. Its second priority is to grow surface roots and search sideways to obtain as much air and nutrients as possible.

A seed-grown root system will extend where needed. A tree grown in a pot or in a field, where it is "root pruned" to form a tight root ball which can be successfully transplanted as a large plant, will have a false beginning because it has as much water, air, and nutrients as it needs and so grows a small root system. As a result, when it is moved into its final home, it will need time to recognize its new scenario and attempt to grow the root system it didn't need while growing in the nursery.

If there is a good mycorrhizal population in the soil, it will compensate for the tree's miniaturized root system. But if it is "unfriendly" soil, then the tree will generally have a shortened life.

This is why the numbers show a 50 percent death rate in the first twenty years of life for city trees, and only a short life (one quarter of their normal life expectancy) for the remaining fifty percent. Seed-sown trees will give us the longevity we want for trees and the resultant cost savings that we all expect and want for the trees we plant both now and in the future.

Landscape architecture and engineering— awareness of roots

Both of these professions are aware that compaction kills trees, but neither profession is given the knowledge to prevent this from happening. Neither profession understands that soil, and the roots which live within it, needs ongoing air exchange for life to exist and to thrive in the hundreds of years that a tree is anticipated to live.

However, both professions are the primary designers of city spaces where trees will be planted and the conditions their root systems will have to exist within. Not designing for the long-term health of root systems is the primary cause of problems for city trees.

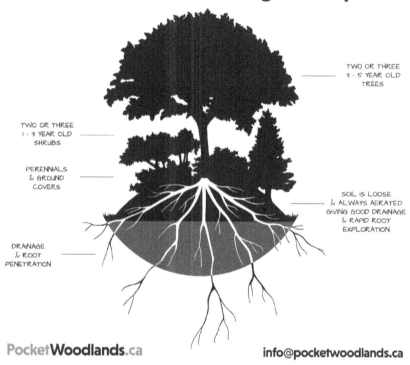

Pocket Woodlands® Design Principles

TWO OR THREE
3 - 5 YEAR OLD
TREES

TWO OR THREE
1 - 3 YEAR OLD
SHRUBS

PERENNIALS
& GROUND
COVERS

SOIL IS LOOSE
& ALWAYS AERATED
GIVING GOOD DRAINAGE
& RAPID ROOT
EXPLORATION

DRAINAGE
& ROOT
PENETRATION

PocketWoodlands.ca

info@pocketwoodlands.ca

Pocket Woodlands aims to cultivate a community of aware citizens around the world to create thriving communities of trees. To support our vision, we have curated a comprehensive Resource Section, on our website, a treasure trove of case studies, articles, and research papers focused on vital aspects of healthy trees, urban tree canopy cover, and tree mortality rates.

Dive into our website's Resources Section for valuable insights on tree health, urban canopy cover, and more. These resources offer educational insights, design inspiration, and evidence-based decision-making tools for both enthusiasts and professionals.

Some especially important articles to consider are:

Mortality rates for people, correlated with the number of urban street trees planted over a 30-year period in Portland, Oregon

www.pocketwoodlands.ca/post/planting-trees-can-save-lives-study-shows

The relationship between tree canopy and crime rates (USDA)

www.pocketwoodlands.ca/post/the-relationship-between-tree-canopy-and-crime-rates-across-an-urban-rural-gradient-in-the-greater-b

Summary of studies on street tree survival rates

www.pocketwoodlands.ca/post/street-tree-survival-rates-meta-analysis-of-previous-studies-and-application-to-a-field-survey-in-p

International Society of Arboriculture review of street tree mortality studies

www.pocketwoodlands.ca/post/urban-tree-mortality-a-literature-review

Explore our website and resources to learn more about what we do.

For more information, contact us at info@pocketwoodlands.ca or visit https://www.pocketwoodlands.ca

Pocket Woodlands® – Inspired by nature, backed by research

Printed in the USA
CPSIA information can be obtained
at www.ICGtesting.com
JSHW011806140924
69673JS00005BA/7